CULTURE

in North & South Korea

Melanie Guile

Raintree
Chicago, Illinois

Library of Congress Cataloging-in-Publication Data
Guile, Melanie.
  North and South Korea / Melanie Guile.
      p. cm. -- (Culture in--)
Summary: Looks at the literature, arts, architecture, and general culture of the countries of North and South Korea.
  ISBN 1-4109-0472-5 (library bdg.-hardcover)
 1. Arts, Korean--Korea (North)--Juvenile literature. 2. Arts, Korean--Korea (South)--Juvenile literature. [1. Arts, Korean--Korea (North) 2. Arts, Korean--Korea (South)] I. Title. II. Series: Guile, Melanie. Culture in--   .
  NX584.7.A1G85 2003
  951.9--dc21   2003005198

J
915.19
GUI
c.1

$19.99

Acknowledgments
The publisher would like to thank the following for permission to reproduce photographs:
pp. 7, 23 © Chris Lisle/Australian Picture Library (APL)/Corbis; p. 8 Australian Picture Library (APL)/Corbis/© AFP; p. 9 Australian Picture Library (APL)/© Corbis; pp. 10, 16, 28, 29 Courtesy of the Korean National Tourist Organisation; p. 11 Kim Jae-Hwan/AFP/AAP; p. 12 Yun Jai-hyoung/© 2002 AP/AAP; p. 13 © Joren Gerhard Australian Picture Library (APL)/Corbis; p. 14 Australian Picture Library (APL)/Corbis/© Bohemian Nomad Picturemakers; p. 15 © Stephanie Maze/Australian Picture Library (APL)/Corbis; p. 17 © Michael Freeman/Australian Picture Library (APL)/Corbis; p. 18 John Elk III/Lonely Planet Images; p. 19 © Michael S. Yamashita/Australian Picture Library (APL)/Corbis; p. 20 © Massimo Mastrorillo/Australian Picture Library (APL)/Corbis; p. 21 GMM; p. 23 (top) PhotoDisc; p. 23 (bottom) By kind permission of the Ho-Am Foundation; p. 27 Australian Picture Library (APL)/Corbis/© ART on FILE; p. 25 (top) © Cardinale Stephane/Australian Picture Library (APL)/Corbis; p. 26 By kind permission of the Korean Cultural Service Library, New York; p. 25 (bottom) The Nostalgia Factory.

Other Acknowledgments
Cover photograph: Yun Jai-hyoung/© 2002 AP/AAP. Bystanders watch a huge dragon-shaped lantern during the Super Lantern Festival, part of the Buddha's Birthday festivities, in South Korea.

Every effort has been made to contact copyright holders of any material reproduced in this book. Any omissions will be rectified in subsequent printings if notice is given to the publisher.

CONTENTS

Some words are shown in bold, **like this**. You can find out what they mean by looking in the glossary.

CULTURE IN
North and South Korea

Extending in a hook shape from the Asian mainland, the Korean peninsula lies between two great powers, China and Japan. The Koreans have absorbed many influences from their neighbors, yet their culture is quite distinct. Their **ancestors** were **nomads** who roamed the grasslands of central Asia. The Korean language has ancient links with the languages spoken by the peoples of Turkey and Mongolia, and it is not related to Chinese. Around 30,000 years ago, these tribal people settled on the Korean peninsula and developed their own rich culture.

What is culture?

Culture is a people's way of living. It is the way in which they identify themselves as a group, separate and different from any other. Culture includes a group's spoken and written language, social customs, and habits, as well as its traditions of art, craft, dance, drama, music, literature, and religion.

Cult of the Kims

In North Korea former leader Kim Il-sung and his son Kim Jong-il—the current leader—have godlike status. Photos of them are displayed in every home, and each citizen must wear a red badge bearing the leader's picture. Every newspaper runs several pictures of the Kims daily. According to some reports, people must cut these pictures out carefully and return them to district collection points. If they are caught throwing them away, they may risk being arrested and sent to prison.

A nation divided

The first Korean kingdom was formed around 100 C.E., and remained one nation until the end of World War II in 1945, when it was divided into two countries—the **communist** north, controlled by the **Union of Soviet Socialist Republics (USSR),** and the south, controlled by the United States. In 1950 the Korean communists invaded the south. The Korean War that followed (1950–1953) involved many nations, especially the United States (which sent forces to assist the South Korean military), and devastated the countryside. Finally, a truce was called. But the country remained divided, and North and South Korea have developed separately for the past 50 years. So the two Koreas share common traditions and language, but daily life in each country is now very different.

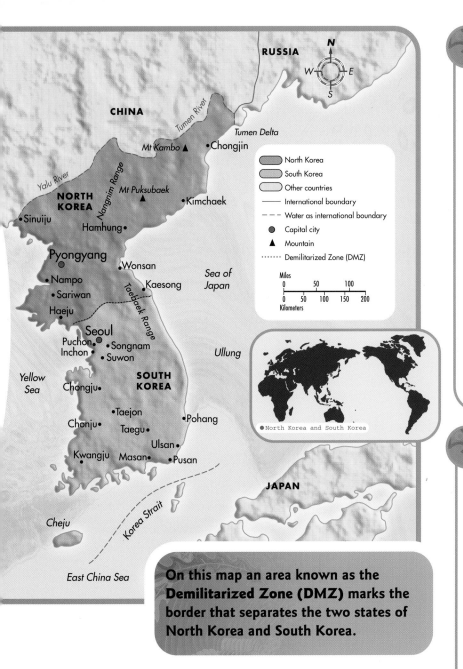

RUSSIA

CHINA

Tumen River

Tumen Delta

Mt Kambo ▲ •Chongjin

•Kimchaek

NORTH
KOREA

Yalu River

Nangnim Range

▲ Mt Puksubaek

•Sinuiju

Hamhung•

Pyongyang

•Wonsan

•Nampo

Kaesong

•Sariwan

Haeju•

Taebaek Range

Seoul
Puchon•
Inchon• •Songnam
         •Suwon

SOUTH
KOREA

Chongju•

•Taejon

Chonju•   Taegu•

•Pohang

Ulsan•

Kwangju• Masan•
          •Pusan

Cheju

East China Sea

Yellow
Sea

Korea Strait

JAPAN

*Sea of
Japan*

Ullung

	North Korea
	South Korea
	Other countries
——	International boundary
– – –	Water as international boundary
●	Capital city
▲	Mountain
····	Demilitarized Zone (DMZ)

Miles
0   50   100
0 50 100 150 200
Kilometers

●North Korea and South Korea

On this map an area known as the Demilitarized Zone (DMZ) marks the border that separates the two states of North Korea and South Korea.

Flag of North Korea

Flag of North Korea

The wide red band on the flag of the Democratic People's Republic of Korea (North Korea) stands for revolutionary spirit. The red star in the circle represents the Korean Workers' Party, which rules the country. The blue is for peace, and the two white bands represent purity.

Flag of South Korea

The white background of the flag of the Republic of Korea (South Korea) represents purity. The round symbol in the middle is a *taeguk*, a Korean version of the Chinese **yin and yang** symbol, represents balance and harmony. The marks in each corner stand for heaven, Earth, water, and fire.

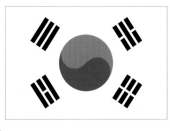

In North Korea the communist government oversees every aspect of people's lives. There is strict **censorship** of the press, which must always cast North Korea in a positive light. Limits are imposed on travel, school, and work choices. All religion is outlawed, and music, drama, literature, and modern styles of painting are strictly controlled. Any influences perceived to be from western, **capitalist** society are prohibited.

While in North Korea the same system of government has remained in place since shortly after World War II, South Korea has had numerous different leaders and versions of its constitution. Today, its government is based on a strongly **democratic** constitution adopted in 1987. South Korea's 48 million people enjoy a healthy economy, a free press, and flourishing arts—both modern and traditional.

South Korea after the Korean War

South Korea impressed the world with its remarkable turnaround after the devastation of the Korean War. It is considered one of the "Asian Tigers"—Asian countries that achieved amazing economic growth after the end of World War II. Its success is due mainly to huge, family-run manufacturing companies called *jaebeol,* which export high-quality South Korean goods worldwide, including cars, computer hardware, electrical appliances, and heavy machinery. Well-known *jaebeol* include Hyundai, LG (Lucky Goldstar), Daewoo, and Samsung. For years, under an oppressive **dictator** named General Park Chung-hee (who ruled South Korea from 1961 to 1979), low-paid workers for these companies labored long hours in poor conditions to build the economy. Now, in spite of an economic downturn during the late 1990s, South Koreans enjoy one of the highest standards of living in Asia.

North Korea after the Korean War

After the end of the Korean War in 1953, North Korea was locked away under the long-term **communist** dictator Kim Il-sung (who ruled from 1948–1994). He developed a theory called the **Juche Idea,** which, among other things, said that North Korea should not rely on any other country for goods or services, but must be totally self-sufficient. Unfortunately, the country could not produce everything its 24 million people needed, leading to shortages of basic food, medicines, and fuel.

With the help of its communist neighbors, China and the **USSR**, industries were established and health clinics and schools were set up. But in the late 1980s, the economy began to collapse after its main communist supporter, the USSR, split apart into separate countries and ceased to exist. Since then, North Koreans have been faced with shortages, widespread poverty, strict **censorship,** and a collapsing economy.

There has always been severe tension between the **capitalist** south and the communist north, but economic hardship has made North Korea more interested in building ties with South Korea. In 2000 the South Korean president, Kim Dae-jung, had a meeting with Kim Il-sung's son, Kim Jong-il, who assumed leadership of North Korea after the elder Kim's death in 1994. It was the first such meeting since the Korean War, and Kim Dae-jung was awarded the Nobel Peace Prize in 2000 for his efforts at **reconciliation.** However, relations between the two countries soured in 2003 after North Korea threatened military strikes against the south.

A Buddhist ceremony in South Korea features offerings of flowers, fruit, and candles.

Religions

Four religions have influenced Korean culture: spirit worship, **Buddhism, Confucianism,** and **Christianity.** In North Korea no religions are openly practiced.

Spirit worship (called **animism** or **shamanism**) dates back to prehistoric times, and centers on the belief that all things in the universe have a soul. In Korea there are currently about 40,000 shamans (priests) called *mudang*, most of whom are women. These *mudang* perform **rituals** to drive out evil spirits and bring good fortune.

Buddhism is based on the life and teachings of Gautama Buddha, known as **the Buddha,** who was born in about 563 B.C.E in India and lived until about 483 B.C.E. Buddhism came to Korea around 300 C.E. It emphasizes leading a pure, simple life in search of a peaceful state called enlightenment.

First introduced to Korea in about the third century B.C.E., Confucianism is a philosophy based on the teachings of an ancient Chinese scholar, Confucius. It teaches that there is a proper order to all things in the universe, including human society. To maintain this order, Confucianism offers guidelines for behavior, emphasizing respect for elders and **ancestors.**

Christianity arrived in Korea in the late 18th century, when missionaries from Europe came to the peninsula. Today 30 percent of South Koreans follow Christianity, making it the second largest religious group in the country after Buddhism.

EVERYDAY LIFE
in North Korea

Since North Korea became a separate **communist** country in 1945, it has been isolated from the rest of the world. Almost no one is allowed in or out, but some have escaped over the Chinese border, bringing stories about the difficulties North Koreans face in their daily lives.

Iron control

The North Korean government distributes food, housing, education, and jobs, and people have no say in where they live or work. All food, clothing, and household goods are given out in set amounts every month. Rice, barley, and vegetables are the main foods. No one may travel within the country without permission, and attempting to leave the country is a crime. Huge prison camps hold as many as 200,000 prisoners who have been jailed for their political views. Most do not survive because of terrible conditions in the camps.

The armed forces

North Korea has an army of over a million—one of the world's largest. There are no official laws about who must join the military, but in reality everyone is expected to serve for up to seven years. Soldiers are often put to work on major government building projects such as roads, dams, and bridges.

A sweeper keeps the street spotless under a statue of Kim Il-sung in North Korea's capital, P'yongyang. The city has an underground train station with marble floors, and the world's highest fountain, 492 feet (150 meters) tall.

Class divisions

In the late 1960s, officials used the results of a survey to group North Koreans into three classes based on their loyalty to the government. The **privileged** Core Group (28 percent of the population) includes high-ranking officials of the communist party and their families. The Unstable Group (45 percent) includes anyone whose loyalty to the state is uncertain, such as low-ranking government employees and other workers. Everyone else is assigned to the Hostile Group (27 percent). Citizens in this group are used for slave labor and denied opportunities for housing, jobs, and education. Only Core Group members are allowed to live in the capital, P'yongyang.

Showy city

When foreign visitors come to P'yongyang, they see a clean, modern city with many lavish monuments. Kim Il-sung designed the capital to make his country appear as successful and powerful as possible. Elderly and disabled people are kept off the streets, and all of the city maps are distorted to make the impressive heart of the city appear bigger than it is.

Family life

About 70 percent of North Koreans live in poverty, working long days in factories or on farms. Private homes generally have two rooms and a courtyard for cooking. People work six days a week, and rest on Sundays with picnics, walks in parks, and other activities. In P'yongyang a popular outing is to view the beautiful lit-up fountains near the Mansudae Art Theater.

Shortages

A terrible food shortage, or famine, gripped North Korea during 1997 and 1998. The international aid organization World Vision estimated that up to 2 million people starved to death. People were allowed only half a cup (100 grams) of rice per day, and most were forced to eat wild leaves and roots to survive. International experts blame the famine on drought, floods, and poor planning by the government.

Along with contributing to food shortages, North Korea's policy against imports has also caused shortages of fuel, household goods, and medicines. In 1999 all public buses outside of P'yongyang were abandoned because there was no gas to run them. Health care is crumbling, too. The Red Cross reported in 2001 that basic medicine and equipment were unavailable at most health clinics.

Members of the Red Cross distribute famine aid to North Korean citizens.

TRADITIONS
and Customs

Vanishing cultures

Both north and south of the **Demilitarized Zone (DMZ),** Korean traditions are in danger of disappearing, but for very different reasons. In wealthy, westernized South Korea, many locals worry that ancient customs are no longer being observed. They feel that traditional values like self-control and politeness are being pushed aside by more casual attitudes imported from the United States and other western countries. In North Korea, on the other hand, old ways have faded because most of them have been banned by the government. Traditional festivals have been replaced with new ones that promote the principles of **communism.** People now celebrate special days for workers, such as Miners' Day, rather than religious holidays like **the Buddha's** Birthday. However, leader Kim Jong-il shows signs of relaxing these rules, and traditions like *Dangun* Festival, which marks the ancient founding of Korea, have quietly crept back.

Personal relationships

Clear rules apply in social relations between Koreans. The most important is maintaining *kibun* (harmonious feelings), which prevents people from embarrassing others in public. The ideas of Confucius, who lived in about 500 B.C.E., also influence life throughout Korea. Confucius set forth rules of behavior for five different types of relationships: master and servant, father and son, husband and wife, young and old, and friends. Loyalty to family and respect for authority are extremely important, and children are expected to obey their parents on matters like dating and careers.

Traditional gender roles

According to **Confucianism** in traditional Korea, women did not have jobs or go to school, and had to obey their husbands and elder sons. **Rituals** honoring **ancestors** were performed only by males. Because sons cared for their parents in old age, girl babies were often unwanted and abandoned at birth.

Children pay respects to their parents at Lunar New Year. Showing respect for elders is an important Korean value.

Women in North and South Korea

Under communism women are regarded as equal to men, so North Korean girls are educated, work on family farms, serve in the army, and are assigned jobs. Even so, women are expected to prepare meals and take charge of the home. This is not an easy task, since frequent shortages mean that women often must gather food and fuel from the wild.

The situation of women in South Korea has improved over the past 50 years. They receive twelve years of schooling and hold jobs, but women still generally have lower pay and less powerful positions than men. There are few female politicians or business executives. Women are expected to perform household duties, and good *kimchi* (pickled cabbage) continues to be a sign of a good housewife.

Taekwondo

Korea's national sport is *taekwondo*, which means "the art of kicking and punching." It developed in Korea more than 2,000 years ago as mental and physical training exercises for soldiers. *Taekwondo* is similar to karate, but it has a stronger emphasis on rapid, athletic kicking with the feet. Like other forms of martial arts, courage, obedience, and self-control are as important as physical strength.

Male culture

The idea of male superiority has deep roots in Korean culture. Korean men identify themselves with the nation's ancient, heroic soldiers, famous for their strength and cunning in battle. Admiral Yi Sun-sin is a national hero in the north and south. In 1592 he defeated a huge Japanese invading navy, sinking 500 of its ships using his new invention—ships armored with iron. Korean men are protective of their women, and frown upon men from western countries marrying Korean women, which has become more common in recent years. Sports in South Korea are also dominated by men, such as hiking, mountain biking, skiing, and the national sport, *taekwondo*.

Throughout Korea most families have just two children. Especially in South Korea, boys are valued more than girls because they are expected to look after their parents in later life, they continue the family lineage, and they contribute to the family finances. In South Korea currently 116 males are born for every 100 females. This shortage of girls has occurred because many parents decide to end the pregnancy if they know the unborn child is female. It is now illegal in South Korea for doctors to tell parents whether their baby is a boy or girl before its birth.

Education

Twelve years of schooling are required in South Korea, and parents and teachers push the pupils very hard. Most children attend after-school tutoring classes, and spend weekends and holidays studying for exams. There is fierce competition for the best schools and universities. In North Korea primary school is compulsory, but top schools and universities are reserved for **Communist** Party officials and their families.

Festivals in South Korea

At Lunar New Year *(Sol)* in January, people try to get together with their relatives and to pay respect to their **ancestors.** Dressed in traditional costumes, younger family members make a deep bow *(sebae)* to their parents and exchange formal greetings as a sign of obedience.

The Harvest Moon Festival *(Chusok),* around September, is South Korea's biggest holiday. Families visit the graves of ancestors and offer prayers to them, bring treats to neighbors, and view the full moon.

All of South Korea lights up at **the Buddha's** Birthday in May. People hang colored paper lanterns with prayers written on them in temples to bring grace to the family. The beautiful Tobongsan monastery, near Seoul, holds prayers at dusk when the lanterns are lit. Some cities hold street parades featuring lanterns as well.

Spectacular lanterns such as this dragon-shaped one take center stage at Buddha's Birthday celebrations in South Korea.

The Wedding Duck

Wedding ducks are given to brides and grooms as traditional tokens of everlasting love and good fortune. Each wooden duck is carved by a family friend and is brought to the ceremony wrapped in colored cloth. The groom's mother throws the duck into the bride's apron. If she catches it, her firstborn will be a son; if she doesn't, it will be a girl. The wedding duck is kept on display at the couple's home.

North Korean holidays

The birthdays of the former North Korean leader Kim Il-sung and his son, Kim Jong-il, are national holidays. They are celebrated with huge military parades and massive shows with dancers, singers, and acrobats. Extra food rations used to be distributed on these occasions as gifts from the leader, but the economic crisis of the 1980s and 1990s put an end to this custom.

Since 1994 the traditional *Dangun* Festival (October 3) has been revived in the north. It celebrates the **myth** of how Korea was founded by Dangun, the son of a god and a bear-woman. Highlights include dancing and singing, games, and the planting of trees.

The Five Fortunes

Traditionally, a Korean man should strive to possess virtues known as the Five Fortunes: wealth, health, no divorces in his family, a good wife, and many sons. Only a man who has the Five Fortunes will be selected to carve the traditional wedding duck for a bride and groom, and he must make only one in his lifetime.

COSTUME
and Clothing

Hanbok

The traditional Korean costume, called *hanbok,* is a symbol of national pride in South Korea. Its design dates back 1,000 years to the Goryeo **Dynasty**, when only the highly educated classes were allowed to wear it. Peasants could wear only simple white clothing, so they became known as "the white-clad people." Today, *hanbok* is worn for festivals and special occasions.

This woman wears *hanbok,* the traditional women's costume in Korea.

Women's *hanbok* consists of a long, very full, high-waisted wraparound skirt called a *chima,* plus a short jacket *(jeogori)* tied at the front with a bow called an *otgoreum.* The bow, with its single loop and dangling ends, must be tied in exactly the right way. Many layers are worn to keep out the winter cold, including loose-fitting underclothes, a full-length underskirt, and a wraparound top.

Men wear baggy pants *(baji)* drawn tight at the ankles, plus a *jeogori* and a long, loose coat *(durumagi).* The most distinctive feature of the men's costume is a black top hat made of horse skin. Traditionally men wore their hair in a bun on the top of their heads, and the hat would sit on top of it. To complete the outfit men slip on shoes with turned-up toes. Both men and women carry drawstring purses called *jumeoni* decorated with elaborate knots and tassels, which originally indicated the wearer's rank.

Color-coded

The colors of clothing once had important meanings in Korea. Unmarried girls wore yellow tops with red skirts; married women wore green jackets. Festivals were occasions for blues, reds, and yellows, colors normally reserved for court ladies. White meant that a person was in mourning.

Everyday clothing in North Korea

Plain western-style clothing is worn in North Korea. Under Kim Il-sung, *hanbok* was banned because it was considered too old-fashioned. Now, however, it is sometimes worn on special occasions. Mao suits (made popular by the **communist** leader of China, Mao Zedong) were once common, but western-style suits (called *yangbok*) are now preferred. Uniforms are required for workers, university students, and government officials.

Everyday clothing in South Korea

In South Korea almost everyone wears western-style clothing, except on special occasions. At weddings traditional *hanbok* is worn by the bride and groom for the ceremony, but the bride often changes into a white dress and veil afterward. Simpler, modern versions of *hanbok* in natural fabrics such as cotton are becoming fashionable for everyday wear.

Men wear traditional outfits at a Confucian ceremony in Seoul, South Korea's capital.

Icinoo

South Korea's best-known fashion designer goes by the name of Icinoo. In 1997 she became the first Korean designer to show a collection in Paris. Her clothing is known for its soft, feminine styles. Icinoo has been called the "grande dame" of Korean fashion, meaning that she is Korea's most important female clothing designer.

FOOD

A zest for spices

Traditional Korean food is hot and zesty, using spices such as chilies, pepper, garlic, ginger, and mustard. Soy sauce, onion, leeks, sesame seeds, and the strong, bitter taste of soybean paste add to the flavors. All meals include steamed rice, soup, and vegetables, with side dishes of fish, pork, chicken, or beef. Koreans eat many vegetables, especially cabbage, green pepper, eggplant, pumpkin, and cucumber. A full traditional Korean meal is called a *hanjoungshik*. It consists of grilled fish, steamed beef ribs, steamed rice, soup, vegetables, and *kimchi*.

Famous dishes

Korea's best-known dish is *kimchi*—a pickled vegetable dish made of cabbage, leeks, or cucumbers spiced with pepper, garlic, and chili, and left to mature in huge jars that are stored outside. *Kimjang* (*kimchi* making) is an important task for Korean homemakers, who must produce enough *kimchi* in autumn to last through the winter.

Bulgogi (which means "fire beef") is often known as Korean barbecue in western countries. It is strips of meat seasoned with soy sauce, garlic, sugar, and sesame oil, and then grilled at the table. Vegetables, chili paste, and plenty of ginger are served with it. *Kujulpan* is a dish for special occasions. Pieces of cooked meat and vegetables are arranged around a central stack of small pancakes, which are then wrapped around a choice of filling.

Bulgogi is often called Korean barbecue in the United States.

Housewives make the traditional pickled vegetable dish *kimchi,* which is known as "the dish that burns twice" because of its spicy flavor.

Mealtimes

It is traditional for a family to sit on the floor around a low table at mealtimes. Soup and rice are served in individual bowls, but all side dishes are shared. Chopsticks are always used, but they are thinner than Chinese ones and made of metal, not wood. People commonly drink barley tea with meals.

Throughout Korea the main meal is usually breakfast, consisting of steamed rice and soup, tofu (soybean curd) or fish, dried seaweed *(gim),* and *kimchi.* Today, though, South Koreans often grab coffee and toast before work, in the western way.

Traditional food

Though it seems shocking to those who think of dogs as pets, dog meat is a traditional food in Korea. This probably came about because people were once forced to eat their hunting dogs in times of famine. Dog is still on the menu in some restaurants, but most Koreans rarely eat it.

PERFORMING ARTS

Rich heritage

Wall paintings in the Tomb of the Dancers, painted around 100 C.E., show that Koreans have enjoyed song and dance since ancient times. In South Korea, performers continue to draw on their rich heritage of music, dance, and other kinds of performance, although western-style dance and music has also become popular. In North Korea, most traditional performing arts are not permitted. The government criticizes traditional music as "impure and depressing." It has invented its own national style of music, based on traditional instruments and songs with political themes.

Listening to South Korean pop music is illegal in North Korea. Acrobatics, however, are encouraged, and the P'yongyang Circus (a famous North Korean acrobatics troupe) offers spectacular athletic entertainment.

Traditional dance

Traditional Korean culture is famous for its great variety of dances. Courtly dances originated as royal entertainment. They are slow and stately, with solemn music and elaborate costumes in the royal colors of yellow, blue, white, red, and black. One example is the Crane Dance, which mimics the graceful movements of two white herons.

Women perform a traditional dance in South Korea.

Foot puppets

Puppetry is an ancient Korean art form. One style, called *palt'al,* uses foot puppets. Performers wear a mask on one outstretched foot. They lie down behind a curtain as they move the puppet's arms using long rods. The stories acted out in puppet shows are usually humorous folktales.

Nong-ak, the unique Farmers' Drum Dance, has been acknowledged by the South Korean government as a national cultural treasure.

Folk dances are for the common people instead of royalty. They are usually very energetic. Among the most famous is the spectacular Farmers' Drum Dance *(nong-ak)*, in which men beat drums strapped around their necks while whirling and leaping. Dancers twirl long streamers attached to their hats, moving quickly and skillfully in time with the drumbeats. Like many folk dances, the *nong-ak* originated as a harvest celebration.

In the Sword Dance *(kommu)*, women hold long swords in both hands and clash them together as they move. A more graceful woman's dance is the *kanggangsuwollae,* in which participants hold hands and chant as they dance in a circle under a full moon. Traditional dances like these are still very popular in South Korea.

Since ancient times Koreans have turned to female **shamans** to help in times of trouble. The shamans' sacred dances are still performed in South Korea. In the *kut,* a **ritual** to drive away evil spirits, the shaman hops and twirls with arms outspread, slowly building up speed until she reaches a trancelike state. Mask dances are comic affairs that make fun of life in courts and monasteries. Striking masks express the characters of the dancers. When the performance ends, audience members start dancing, too.

"Flower of Korea"

Choe Sung-hee (1911–1967) took up dance when she was fifteen, and went on to become Korea's most famous dancer. In 1927 her ballet solo "Serenade" performed in Seoul made her an overnight sensation. She became known as the "Flower of Korea" and was considered one of the top ten dancers in the world. Because she supported the ideals of **communism,** she moved to North Korea in 1946. There she continued her work in the Choe Sung-hee Dance Research Institute, where she studied traditional dances. The South Korean government could not forgive her for moving to the north, and for years it was illegal even to mention her name in South Korea. However, after her unjust execution by the communist government in 1967, South Koreans were outraged. Today, she is once again a hero in South Korea, and is remembered as the person who saved traditional dance for future generations to enjoy.

Traditional music

Two traditional music styles exist in Korea. *Chongak* is the music of the royal courts. It has a slow, calm beat and is performed on instruments such as the twelve-stringed *kayagum*, a two-stringed violin called a *haegum*, and a drum *(changgo)*. Wooden flutes, gongs, and cymbals are also featured in traditional orchestras. A kind of folk music called *minsogak* uses the same instruments but is much livelier.

P'ansori is an art form that combines music and drama. It features one singer/storyteller accompanied by a single drummer, who makes comic remarks about the story being told. Performances last up to eight hours and are based on folktales such as the sad "Tale of Simchong," also known as "The Blind Man's Daughter," in which a young girl sacrifices herself for her father. A variation on *p'ansori* is *ch'ang*. It has a large cast of singers who perform different parts and an orchestra. In South Korea the National Ch'ang Troupe, established in the early 1960s, specializes in this classic form of storytelling.

Music in the family

Chung Kyung-wha is one of the world's finest violinists. With 32 recordings to her credit, she enjoys an international audience, and was awarded South Korea's highest honor, the Civil Merit Medal. Her sister is also an accomplished musician and member of the acclaimed classical cello, violin, and piano group, the Chung Trio. Her younger brother, Chung Myung-whun, is a world-famous pianist and conductor who was named Man of the Year by **UNESCO** in 1995. He currently represents his country around the world as South Korea's cultural **ambassador.**

This woman plays a traditional stringed instrument.

Music in South Korea today

Many South Koreans have achieved international fame in western classical music.
Soprano Kim Won-jung is an international singing star and has her own TV show.
Choirs are very popular, and Korea won first prize at the World Chorus Competition
in Vienna in 1997. The National Opera Group performs both western works and new
Korean operas, and 31 symphony orchestras across the country draw large audiences.

The sweet, innocent image of the band
Baby Vox is typical of female K-pop stars.

K-pop

South Korean pop music (also known as K-pop or *gayo*) is all the rage throughout Asia.
K-pop, like most Asian pop music, tends to be soft and sweet without the harsh rock
sounds of western pop music, but rap is also very big. Many pop stars (called *gasoos*)
are former models, and white bleached hair for male performers is considered stylish.

Until they split up in 2000, Korea's most popular band was a group called HOT. One
member, KangTa, is now a solo star with his own radio show. The all-female band Baby
Vox is also very popular, and Shin Hwa, an all-male rap-pop band, has fans all over Asia.

LITERATURE

Ancient works

The earliest existing Korean book is *Samguk Sagi (Historical Record of the Three Kingdoms)*, written in 1146 C.E. by historian Kim Pusik. *Samguk Yusa (Memories of the Three Kingdoms)* is a book of Korean **myths** and legends, written in the 1200s by the **Buddhist** priest Iryon. It includes the legend of how *Dangun* (half-man, half-sun god) founded the Korean people. Both these classics were produced during a golden age of Korean history known as the **Three Kingdoms period** (about 200–600 C.E.) when the arts flourished. These works of literature were written in Chinese characters because Korean writing was not invented until the 1450s.

Korean classics

The first novel written in *Hangul*, the Korean language, was *The Story of Hong Kiltong* by Ho Kyun (1569–1618), in which a bandit hero founds an ideal society on Yul Island. Korea's most famous love story is *The Story of Ch'unhyang*, about a noble youth's tragic love for an entertainer's daughter and their struggles to be together. This folktale was based on real people who lived during the Choson **Dynasty** (beginning 1392).

Eighty thousand wooden blocks were carved to print the book *Tripitaka Koreana*, one of Korea's most famous national treasures.

Tripitaka Koreana

The Koreans learned how to print books from the Chinese, who invented a method of printing using carved wooden blocks in around 800 C.E. In 1237 a classic book of Buddhist thoughts and beliefs known as the *Tripitaka Koreana* was printed in Korea. The job took fifteen years and required more than 80,000 woodblocks.

Hangul alphabet

Korean writing looks somewhat like Chinese, but it is really closer to English and other **phonetic** languages. Originally Korean was written down in Chinese characters (which represent the meanings of words, not their sounds), and only scholars could write it. *Hangul* was invented by King Sejong in 1446. It gave Koreans their own written language and made writing accessible to ordinary people. Each word resembles a Chinese character (picture-word), but in fact is made up of letters and syllables arranged in a square pattern, not in a line as in English words. There are 24 letters in *Hangul*, and it is written from left to right.

Modern literature

In 1884, after years of isolation from the rest of the world, Korea opened its doors to foreign influences. New European ideas led writers to try different kinds of stories. The most well-known of these more modern and realistic novels is probably Tears *of Blood* (1906) by Yi Injik. *Peace Under Heaven,* by Ch'ae Mansik (written in 1937), introduced a lovable rascal named Master Yun, one of Korea's most famous characters from a book.

The Korean War and the separation of the country into two parts led writers from north and south to take different paths. North Korean writing is strictly controlled by the government, and most works are **propaganda.** The same was true in the south under General Park in the 1960s and 1970s, although this period still produced some fine books. The famous novel *The Land* (1970), by Pak Kyong-ri, is about a landowning family and the clash of old and new cultures. This best-seller has been made into a TV series in South Korea. Today's most famous writer in South Korea is Yi Munyol, whose novel *Our Twisted Hero* (1987) won him a prestigious national award and was recently published in the United States.

Sijo poetry

Sijo is similar to the *haiku* poetry of Japan. *Sijo* poems are 3 lines long and consist of 45 syllables. The beauty of nature is a common theme, and the last line of most *sijo* contains a twist of meaning that brings the poem to a close.

South Korea's most famous modern writer, Yi Munyol (left), receives an award for his books in 1999.

FILM

and Television

North and South Korea's film and television industries are vastly different. In the north the government controls all content and uses the media to reinforce its political ideals. South Korea has a thriving independent film industry, aided by a law that requires at least 40 percent of the movies shown in theaters to be made by Koreans. Television programs are very similar to those made in the United States and elsewhere in the West, and news reports are not restricted.

Television in North Korea

There is one television channel in North Korea, which is run by the government and broadcasts for a few hours daily. Programs highlight state achievements—for example, they might show the "Dear Leader" Kim Jong-il touring a factory or watching a military parade. Other programs celebrate how important workers are to North Korean society. They are portrayed as heroes performing feats such as running with boulders strapped to their backs to build a dam. Feature films made in India are sometimes shown on television to provide entertainment. Very little information from the outside world reaches North Korean citizens because the government has such strict control over the media.

Television in South Korea

Four networks and several cable channels offer a great variety of programs. Dramatic series are hugely popular, such as a soap opera called *Endless Love* about two baby girls switched at birth. Soap opera stars attract crowds of fans at home as well as in Taiwan and Japan. Action-packed kung fu shows like *Flying Dragon* also rate well. After years of strict **censorship** under military dictator General Park, television journalists can now report news freely.

Film

North Korean films are not shown outside the country, so little is known about them. The government provides money to produce **propaganda** films, which are made to promote political points of view rather than to entertain people. As with the programs made for TV, these films usually feature heroic workers fighting against the influences of western, **capitalist** culture. It is believed that these films are technically well made.

South Korean film director Im Kwon Taek (center) is pictured here with actors Cho Seung Woo and Lee Hyo Jong.

The Father of New Korean Cinema

Director Im Kwon-taek (born 1936) is South Korea's most famous filmmaker. Since 1962 he has directed more than 100 films, such as *Surrogate Woman* (1986), and the successful *Sopyonje* (1993). In 2002 Im Kwon-teak achieved international fame when his film *Chihwaseon (Strokes of Fire)*, about the famous 19th-century painter Jang Seung-up, was awarded the prize for Best Director at the Cannes Film Festival.

South Korean films are currently gaining international attention. They tend to feature plenty of action and special effects, although more complex characters and storylines are becoming more common. In 1999 director Song Il-gon's short film, *The Picnic,* won the Jury Prize at the famous Cannes International Film Festival. *Shiri* (1999), directed by Kang Je-gyu, is a spy thriller about a North Korean **terrorist** plot. It starred Korea's highest-paid actor, Han Suk-gyu, and broke box office records in South Korea.

Southern stars

South Korea's most famous actress is Kang Su-youn (born 1966). She won Best Actress in 1987 at the Venice Film Festival for her role in Im Kwon-teak's drama, *Surrogate Woman*. Ahn Sung-ki (born 1952) is an experienced actor who has performed in 53 films. He won his first international acting award in 1960 at the age of seven for his role in a movie called *The Teenagers' Rebellion*. His performance in the 2002 film *Chihwaseon,* about a famous Korean artist, helped win the film one of the top awards at the Cannes Film Festival. Park Joong-hoon (born 1964) is one of a new generation of actors. He studied film in the United States and starred in many hits at home, including the suspenseful *Nowhere to Hide* (1999). He is now an international star and recently appeared in the 2002 Hollywood movie, *The Truth About Charlie.*

This poster advertised the 1999 movie *Nowhere to Hide,* starring Park Joong-hoon.

25

Arts and crafts in Korea were strongly influenced by neighboring China and Japan. However, Korean artistic styles developed over time to be less elaborate than China's, and more playful and informal than those of Japan.

Traditional painting

Uniquely Korean styles of art emerged for the first time during the Choson **Dynasty** (1392–1910). One of these styles was genre painting, in which artists depict lifelike, colorful scenes from everyday life, in contrast to the more tranquil Chinese landscapes. Kim Hong-do (1745–1818) was the

most famous of these genre painters. Another popular painting form was the "Four Gracious Plants" style, featuring plum blossom, orchids, bamboo, and chrysanthemums, all symbols of good fortune in **Confucianism.**

Korean traditional folk paintings *(minhwa)* are also well known today. *Minhwa* painters were untrained and did not sign their works. They used rough, simple techniques and their subjects were usually light-hearted or comical. Popular folk art subjects were landscapes, hunting scenes, flowers, and birds, as well as traditional scenes of a tiger sitting under a pine tree with a magpie in it.

This traditional folk painting (minhwa) features two popular subjects: a tiger and a magpie. The tiger is an important character in Korean folklore, and usually plays the role of a kind, friendly guardian. The magpie represents good luck.

Folk-art sculptures

Throughout South Korea's countryside, you will see simple figures carved in granite, guarding village and town gateways. These are spirit **totems,** placed to bring protection or good luck to the townspeople. Figures include smiling boys, animals, **Buddhist** symbols, and pagodas. A wealthy travel agent named Chun Shin-il began collecting these sculptures twenty years ago to preserve them. In 2000 he opened Sejoong Stone Museum in Seoul, which houses more than 10,000 examples of this ancient art form.

This unusual piece of modern sculpture is by the world-famous artist Paik Nam-june. Called *Small Figure Watching Television*, it comes from a larger work with a television theme. It was created for the University of California at San Diego, where it is located near a media center.

Western-style art

Exposure to foreign artwork in the late 1800s led Korean artists to experiment with European styles. They began to use color and shading in addition to simple lines and started painting in a more realistic way. Jang Seung-up (1843–1897), known as Ohwon, was world famous for the beauty of his delicate paintings. His difficult life is dramatized in Im Kwon-taek's prize-winning film, *Chihwaseon*. Kim Whan-ki (1913–1974) pioneered modern **abstract** art in Korea. He founded an artistic movement called "New Realism," which blended an abstract style with traditional Korean subjects. For example, there are mountains, birds, and flowers in his painting, *An Everlasting Song* (1957), but they appear on a flat, unrealistic background.

Paik Nam-june (born 1932) is regarded as one the world's greatest living artists. He shocked South Koreans with early works such as *Klavier Integral* (1960), in which a piano is decorated with objects such as barbed wire, toys, eggshells, and women's underwear. In the 1980s he became famous for his television sculptures, such as *Video Fish* (1975), in which 54 television sets were arranged behind 54 fish tanks. Recently he has experimented with animation, computer graphics, and lasers. Paik Nam-june now lives in New York City.

Modern art in North Korea

Strict rules are enforced about what artists can paint in North Korea. Acceptable subjects are war scenes, heroic workers and farmers, and portraits of the two Kims. North Korea's most successful artist is Kim Tong-hwan, who works in P'yongyang's Mansudae Art Studio. His paintings include the best-known portrait of Kim Jong-il. In 1998 Kim Tong-hwan was awarded the title "Labor Hero," North Korea's highest honor.

Crafts

Over their 2,000-year history, Korean **artisans** developed many skills in metalwork, jewelry making, granite stone sculpture, papermaking, pottery, and embroidery. However, war and Japanese invasion from the 1400s to the 1600s caused most of these ancient skills to be lost. After the country was divided in 1953, South Koreans made a determined effort to rediscover traditional craft techniques. In North Korea the government prides itself on its collections of traditional handcrafts.

Decorative embroidery is used extensively for wall hangings and traditional costumes in Korea. Selected designs have been named "Important Intangible Cultural Assets" by the South Korean government. This is a special category for concepts or customs (as opposed to specific objects) that are considered uniquely Korean.

Celadon—the pride of Korea

Since around 900 C.E. Korean porcelain (known as celadon or green jade pottery) has been prized throughout Asia. Porcelain is a lightweight, white china with a hard, shiny surface called a glaze. It was invented by the Chinese around 600 C.E. Koreans adapted it by creating a soft green glaze with a crackle finish that gives a beautiful glossy finish to the pots. They made simple but elegant shapes and decorated the surface with patterns using a secret technique. Traditional patterns included dragons (representing power), flowers (health), and cranes (long life). Magnificent celadon pottery was made for use in the royal court and in Buddhist temples during the Koryo **Dynasty** (918–1392), but the skill was lost in the turmoil of Mongol invasions that occurred in about 1400.

After 1400 a less-sophisticated type of pottery called *bun-cheong* replaced the more luxurious celadon. *Bun-cheong* is light brown and white as opposed to green and is roughly decorated with rope or flower patterns. The Japanese invaded Korea in 1592, kidnapped most of the country's master potters, and took them back to Japan to improve the porcelain industry there. After that Korea lost its place as maker of the finest porcelain in Asia. Today, however, South Korean master potters have revived the art of celadon, creating pieces almost as fine as the originals.

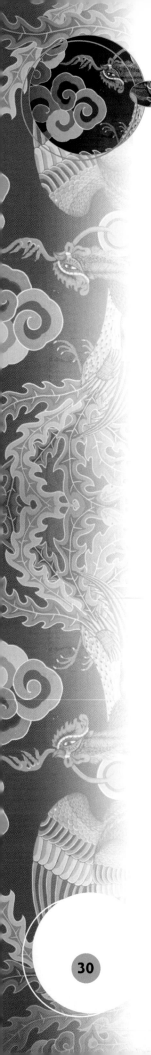

GLOSSARY

abstract in artwork, a style of painting that is not realistic and uses shapes and colors to express emotions or to symbolize ideas

ambassador representative from one country to another

ancestor person from whom one is descended

animism religion in which followers believe that all things in the universe, living and nonliving, have a soul or spirit

artisan person who is highly skilled at making crafts

Buddha, the founder of Buddhism, Gautama Buddha (563 B.C.E.–483 B.C.E.)

Buddhism religion in which followers study the teachings of the Buddha and strive for a peaceful state called enlightenment. A follower of Buddhism is a Buddhist.

capitalist relating to a form of society that has an economy based on the buying and selling of goods for individual profit

censorship practice of preventing certain ideas or information from being freely communicated to the public

Christianity religion based on the belief in one God and the teachings of Jesus, as written in a holy book called the Bible. A follower of Christianity is called a Christian.

communist belonging to a communist political party or having a government based on the ideas of communism. In communism, the government controls all property and industry, and provides each citizen with food, housing, and jobs.

Confucianism religion based on the ideas of the ancient Chinese philosopher, Confucius (551–479 B.C.E.)

Demilitarized Zone (DMZ) space between two enemy countries where no military activity may occur, such as the area between North and South Korea

democratic relating to democracy, a form of government in which decisions are made by elected representatives

dictator single ruler with complete power over a country

dynasty period in which a country has a series of rulers from the same family

Juche Idea principle of economic self-reliance adopted by North Korean leader Kim Il-sung in the 1940s. It ended trade with other countries and resulted in widespread shortages, as North Korea was not able to produce everything it needed on its own.

myth ancient story that tries to explain how aspects of the world came to be

nomad person who roams from place to place without ever settling, usually following seasonal food supplies for flocks or herds

phonetic spelled out using letters to represent the sounds of a spoken language

privileged given special rights or benefits

propaganda materials (such as posters, brochures, or movies) that promote a set of beliefs or ideas to the public

reconciliation process of making peace between former enemies

ritual religious tradition or ceremony

shaman name for a priest or spiritual guide in some religions

shamanism religion in which followers believe that all things in the universe, living and nonliving, have a soul or spirit. Priests called shamans serve as the connection between humans and the spirit world.

terrorist relating to the deliberate use of violence against innocent people to inspire fear for political purposes

totem carved image of a sacred spirit

Three Kingdoms period period in Korean history from 57 B.C.E. to 668 C.E., during which three culturally similar kingdoms existed on the Korean peninsula. This period was marked by strong Chinese influences and the arrival of Buddhism in 372 C.E.

UNESCO (United Nations Educational, Scientific, and Cultural Organization) group that fosters international cooperation in education, science, and culture

Union of Soviet Socialist Republics (USSR) former Russian Communist empire, also known as the Soviet Union, which included Russia and fourteen other republics. The USSR split apart into separate nations in 1991.

yin and *yang* opposite forces present in the universe, which people in many different Asian cultures believe must be in balance for harmony and good health

.FURTHER
Reading

Burgan, Michael. *The Korean War.* Chicago: Heinemann, 2003.

Connor, Mary E. *The Koreas: A Global Studies Handbook.* Santa Barbara, Calif.: ABC-CLIO, 2002.

Curry, Linda S. *A Tiger by the Tail and Other Stories from the Heart of Korea.* Edited by Chan-eung Park. Portsmouth, N.H.: Teacher Ideas Press, 1999.

Olmstead, Mary. *World Tour: Korea.* Chicago: Raintree, 2003.

Shepheard, Patricia. *South Korea.* Broomall, Penn.: Chelsea House, 1999.

INDEX